PLOT

PLOT

Claudia Rankine

Grove Press / New York

The author is grateful to the editors of the following publications, in which sections from PLOT have appeared: *Boston Review, jubilat, Pierogi Press, Poetry Project Newsletter, TriQuarterly*, and *Verse*.

I would like to thank all my friends who read and commented on this manuscript. And for their undying enthusiasm and encouragement I would like especially to thank Sarah Blake, Calvin Bedient, Laure-Anne Bosselaar, Christine Hume, Beverly Rose, Sarah Schulman, and, most especially, my husband, John Lucas. My gratitude to Richard Howard.

Published simultaneously in Canada
Printed in the United States of America

FIRST EDITION

Library of Congress Cataloging-in-Publication Data
Rankine, Claudia, 1963–
    Plot / by Claudia Rankine.
      p. cm.
    ISBN 0-8021-3792-X
    I. Title.
    PS3568.A572 P58 2001
    813'.54—dc21   00-051389

DESIGN BY LAURA HAMMOND HOUGH

Grove Press
841 Broadway
New York, NY 10003

01 02 03 04 10 9 8 7 6 5 4 3 2 1

FOR MARGRETHE WINSLOW

PLOT

:

inverse

1

Submerged deeper than appetite

she bit into a freakish anatomy. the hard plastic of filiation.
a fetus dream. once severed. reattached. the baby femur
not fork-tender though flesh. the baby face now anchored.

What Liv would make would be called familial. not foreign.
forsaken. She knew this. tried to force the scene. focus the
world. in the dream. Snapping, the crisp rub of thumb to index.
she was in rehearsal with everyone. loving the feel of cartilage.
ponderous of damaged leaves. then only she. singing internally.
only she revealed. humming. undressing a lullaby: *bitterly,*
bitterly, sinkholes to underground streams. . . .

In the dream waist deep. retrieving a fossilized pattern forming
in attempt to prevent whispers. or poisoned regrets. reaching into
reams and reams. to needle-seam a cord in the stream. as if
a wish borne out of rah-rah's rude protrusion to follow the rest
was sporded. split. and now hard pressed to enter the birth.

In the dream the reassembled desire to conceive wraps the
tearing placenta to a walled uterus. urge formed complicit. First
portraying then praying to a womb ill-fitting. she grows fat.

The drive in utero is fiction-filled. arbiter of the cut-out infant.
and mainstreamed. Why birth the other. to watch the seam rip.
to roughly conjoin the lacerating generations? Lineage means
to step here on the likelihood of involution. then hard not
to notice the depth of rot at the fleshy roots. To this outbreak
of doubt. she crosses her legs. the weight of one thigh on the
next. constructed rectitude. the heavy. heavy. devotion of no.

Ersatz

outside of this insular traffic a woman in pink underlining the
alias gender. who is she really? call her. could you. would
you. call her. Mommy?

The hope under which Liv stood.

her craven face. it clamored. The trumpeter announced it.
She stood more steady then. marveling at her stammering.
hammering heart. collecting a so-invisible breath. feeling
extreme. commencing. deeper than feeling was.

She wanted what he had been told she'd want. what she was.
expecting. Then the expecting was also a remembering.
remembering to want. She was filling her mouth up with his—

yet it was not. it was not. the sound of sucking on the edge of
sleep. not soft brush of cheek. not the heat of the hand along
the neck.

There is a depiction. picture. someone else's boy gorgeously
scaled down. and crying out. and she not hearing. not having.
not bearing Ersatz—

She was filling her mouth up with his name. yet it was not.
it was not.

Liv forever approaching the boy like toddler to toy. the
mothering more forged than known. the coo-coo rising air
bubbles to meet colostrum. yellow. to blue. to milk. not having
to learn. knowing by herself. Come closer—

in front the glare. pools in straining veins making Liv
nervy. malachite half-moons on each lobe listening inward.
the hormonal trash heap howling back.

There is dust from a filed nail. the wind lifts. carries it into
available light: not monochromatic. not flattened though
isolating. solicitous. soliciting. Come closer—

Once Liv thought pregnancy would purify. You Ersatz
effacing. her pace of guilt. her site of murmur.

Then of course. of course. when do we not coincide elsewhere
with the avoided path? a sharp turn toward the womb-shaped
void? now

Liv is feeling in vitro. duped. a dumbness of chimes. no
smiles for every child so careful. so careful.

Ersatz

infant. bloomed muscle of the uterine wall. you still pink
in the center. resembling the saliva-slick pit of the olive.
resembling tight petals of rose. assembling

Ersatz

This. his name was said. Afterward its expression wearing
the ornate of torment. untouched by discretion. natural light
or (so rumored

(and it. once roused. caused ill-ease as if kissed full on the
mouth.

Herself assaulting the changing conditions, Liv added
desire's stranglehold. envisaged its peculiarly pitched ache
otherwise alien to her wildly incredulous hopes: Ersatz

Ersatz

aware of your welt-rising strokes. your accretion of theme. Liv
was stirring (no. breathing the dream. She was preventing a trust
from forming. still the bony attachment was gaining its tissue
like a wattle-and-daub weave.

Ersatz

arrival is keyhole-shaped. it allows one in the assembled warren
of rooms. to open the game box even as the other leans against
the exposed from her freestanding. exaggerated perspective.

She is on her way in the corridor unable to enter this room
and if she prays to be released from you. as one would
pray to be released from tinnitus or welt. boy ridge of flesh
raised by a blow.

imagine in your uncurl of spinal arch. her eye your eye. an
apparition hushed to distortion. her heart unclosed. yet warped
by dullness and pure feeling. her lips but a crease recrossing
time. needing a softer tone.

Imagine the prayer itself

Ersatz

unswallowed. swollen within her lips. so grieved:

Ersatz,

Here. Here. I am here

inadequately and feeling more and more less so because of not
feeling more, but stopped. For I am of course frightened of you,
what your bold face will show me of me. I am again leading to
regret. I have lived, Ersatz, the confusion in my head, the fusion
that keeps confusion. Could it keep you? Could it make those
promises to remedy tortuous lines, thickening encroachings?

Oh, Ersatz, my own, birth is the limiting of the soul, what is
trapped with it already owns. I could quadruple my intent
toward you, be your first protection; but I could not wish a self
on any self as yet unformed, though named and craved.

Ersatz,

I am here. And here is not analogous to hope.

See past the birth into these eyes of yours, into what
increasingly overstates resemblance, a semblance one might wish
to tuck under, into the sweat of the armpit, into its wiry odor
of exhaustion, remembering the self and any reflection thereof
is never a thing to cradle.

Ersatz,

were I coward enough to have you, child, coward enough to take
my pain and form it into a pulsing, coming round the corner any
odd day, of course, of course, I would believe you the intruder,
had intruded.

Provoked, Ersatz, the best I could be would be shivering illness, mucus rising, the loud rush, the sob.

I am made uncomfortable and more so, no warmer, no closer to the everyone you are. Already the orphan, suffocating and overlapping a trillion faces—

are you utterly anywhere. have we, have we arrived anywhere.

Ersatz,

has the rudimentary ear curled open. are you here?

The Extended Root

What comes through the bloodstream to be flushed reduces him
to human even as he does not breathe, even as his lids lower to
this thick beginning, one-third of an inch below the upper
surface of her swirling pit. The place he fills fills with viscid fuel
and yet, somehow, does not drown him in the basement
membrane of her own convoluted, veined, capillary network,
her own ocean of wear. Nourished, coaxed forward in the
presence of her whole presence, consequence of her con-
sequences, he is blister of cell, grain named embryo, a climbing
substance perceived, absorbing such intimacy as she can offer.

Ersatz   of freehand sketchiness   of hollow form

anonymous   delineation of bone

of moody hue dipped in fetal city   oh so neatly laid

within Liv   estranged interlacing   that she is

Are such seasoned movements truly without desire? Is her
organized breath simply indirection as his face forms in his
eggplant-purple landscape, the likeness of no other? There now
is the peculiar sound of blood flowing, a soft, pulpy *whoosh*,
aquatic, the spreading heart-shaped mouth opening into its
initialed script. Darkly stained, untidy eyebrows, a mole,
blemish-shaped. In the mind's eye never abandoned are the
supposed markings on the boy. What is seen before his profile
splinters is a face that looks and is certainly startled.

How not to smile out loud?

Erland

how not to? when in utero a fetus heartbeat bounces off.
scanned vibrations of this newer soul making a self whole.

how not to? as the chilled gel brings to the screen inked in.
black and white. glimpsed. scrutinized. joy.

Erland

considers this ersatz image. abracadabra and like. so like.
so liked.

by him whose blush tinges with alleluias. so close to life. his
dried lips licked repeatedly.

He's breathing within. but breathless in the red of the ribbon-
cutting. a sunrise.

tickling giddy goodness extracting arrival. here. here is a slip
of fate from a touch that felt right all over.

Erland

in the volumetric space that is him and spilling to become sun-
drenched. impossibly tender.

turning to Liv, love, stands in her way in tinted glasses wanting
slowly to be

received by her who feels survival. its pencil movements.

even as she moves through the still traffic debating.

assuaging doubt.

What do you mean, are we sure?
Just because we are pregnant doesn't mean we have to have it.
What would we be waiting for?
I don't know . . . to be sure?
Liv, are you saying you don't want to have this child?
No . . . no, I am not saying anything. I mean I am just saying we
     could still think about this a little. We still have time.
Time for what? That is what I am not understanding . . .
Time to understand how completely, completely changed our
     lives will be.
Well . . . sure it's scary and things will change, but we will have
     our lives plus the baby. Others have done it. How are we so
     different?
Look, if I can't talk to you about this, who am I to talk to?
I'm sorry I'm happy. I think it will be great. I don't know what
     else to say.

Coherence in Consequence

Imagine them in black, the morning heat losing within this day
that floats. And always there is the being, and the not-seeing on
their way to—

The days they approach and their sharpest aches will wrap
experience until knowledge is translucent, the frost on which
they find themselves slipping. Never mind the loose mindless
grip of their forms reflected in the eye-watering hues of the
surface, these two will survive in their capacity to meet,
to hold the other beneath the plummeting, in the depths below
each step full of avoidance. What they create will be held up,
will resume: the appetite is bigger than joy. indestructible.
for never was it independent from who they are. who will be.

Were we ever to arrive at knowing the other as the same pulsing
compassion would break the most orthodox heart.

2

A short narrative of breasts and wombs entitled

Liv Lying on the Floor Looking at

the Dirty Thought

[The womb similar to fruit that goes uneaten will grow gray fur, the breasts a dying rose, darkening nipples, prickling sickness as it moves toward mold, a spongy moss.]

Liv, answer me this: Is the female anatomically in need of a child as a life preserver, a hand, a hand up? And now, pap smeared, do you want harder the family you fear in fear of all those answers?

Could you put fear there as having to do with him? think. think . . . as having to do with milk? To your health! Cheers. Or against the aging body unused, which way does punishment go?

"Let us not negotiate out of fear. . . ." butbutbut. . . . Then the wind touched the opened subject until Liv in a light breeze, squalls, was without a place to put her ladder.

From the treetop something fell, a bundle, a newspaper, a bug, a bag, still nobody's baby. Sound was desperation dropped down, a falling into place, and not way away—

Statistics show: One in what? One in every what? A child in every pot will help the body grow? No matter, all the minutes willingly slip into the first, then the ashes still shiver.

Liv, is the graffitied mind sprained? Who sprayed a cancer there? Which answer? What dirtied up prevention? No matter. Anyway, which way does your ladder go?

Toward? Or away? in keeping with that ant crawling on your ankle. O mindless hand, rub hard. Not quite in pain because pain is shorthand for what? One in every what? Cradle call.

Ohh kiss it up without facing yourself. Knowing the issue, go ahead, slouch, rest your chin on your folded hands. Think: blunt impact, injury. Toss a "but" against the wall,

tic, tock

10:12 pm

Is it allowed? Am I, as a descendent of particulars, unneeded
times, permitted the thing and more? This world, its worst is real.
What doesn't hurt, ticking past, what doesn't intersect? Our
destinations recalled, our points of fracture, of limbs crushed to
memory, no more than experience, I am too aware of other ways.

Another Frame of Mind

As if a source exists only for its result, within Liv's sketches
lives the eternal term disappearing into her child: mother coded
for other, a gate only, a mighty fortress, a door swinging open . . .

or is she that—that vessel, filling up, swelling to overflow until
mothery is the drowned self, drowning all that is, all that clings?

Whether her eyes are open or closed she hears only a child.
Whether her eyes are open or closed she hears only the child.
Whether her eyes open or close she sees only her child.
Whether her eyes are open or closed she sees only her own. . . .

Or too soon whose womb rhymes with plot? Whether her eyes
are open or closed she feels the same loss in jubilation.

11:26 pm

In the weeks it has taken to suck and swallow, girdled child in the preliminary of tissue, in the rudimentary of ear, of eye, of mouth, why wish to be born? The story remains numb within hunger, the story is occupied pain, the body brims from cracks unnamed. A billion results, each the gulf of a particular break.

Still Life

A draft enters. A sketchy gust. Blown is the woman standing within her likeness. To her left the sun needs to be drawn but her hands are the shape cradling her breasts, keeping her nipples in place. Each breast is the rest floating within metonymy. Her swollen scape keeps her awake. In its milky silence she feels distaste. She holds still. She waits. The draft draws dust into her eyes. Her eyes tear until her outline dislodges. dilutes. blurs.
In the time it takes to fix her face the moon is drawn quartered.

12:13 am

Shaped to this world, its intrinsic illness, maligned by memory, less and less unable to grieve, am I the lot on whom you strive? What is it we are meant to be? Are we love? Are we happiness? Are we truth?

Milk and Tears

Long after she grows tired in the night she hears only the child's
cries. His cries, already recalling, and silence,
the dumbness she wedges herself into.   Cowardly,
and additionally compromised, she hears each cry, punctuating
every space of exception, running through her, meaning to break,
to interrupt each moment attempted. She hears and calls it
silence. Then it is as if the hood of motherhood was meant to
blur herself from herself, a dark cloth dropping over her eyes
until the self of selfless near arose.

1:07 am

Today I wake, tomorrow I wake, and still this assemblage, its
associated distortions, bewilders me.

No Solace from the TV

She said she thought it was a dead animal, some wild animal,
"You know, small animal, killed and buried or . . . or something."
She didn't know. Just not. . . .

She said, "Who would believe that!" She was a woman, she
understood women. This she didn't understand. "As a woman, as
a mother . . . no, this was not . . . not a mother."

"You could see, anyone could see she was pregnant. We aren't
fools. She can't fool anyone. She was pregnant. Where is the
baby?"

"It's hard to know," he said, "hard to know now the
psychological state of the mother. We could be looking at
anything from reckless endangerment to . . . to murder. Intent to
murder. But who knows, you know . . . who knows."

"Someone . . . someone could be thinking a . . . female with a
problem just looking to get rid of the problem. You know, scared
of the equation."

"One could see that this life . . . in this life she might have felt
driven to it . . . without choice. A mother, but not a mother really.
A woman, but not a mother. A desperate woman or perhaps a
woman only."

In the drift from screen to sleep Liv finds no peace. A woman but not a woman really, in her nightmare she chews at her breasts. Hers is the same sucking sound baby goats make. She examines her flesh-toned spit and molds it into sunglasses. After wearing the glasses for some time, her vision, she notes, is angled downward, cradled by a shadow barely a foot long.

The Dream Play

Simultaneously and as a consequence, Erland comes to Liv in her dream. His face is flushed. Has he been running?

Where's the baby? he asks.
I haven't got it, she says.
What's in your stomach then?
The blood's run out.
The blood's run out? Where out?
Out, out, and it's taken the thing with it.
Are you mad?
Don't talk about it.
Where's the baby? he shouts.

The Dream Riddle

If the floor muscle gives way, bitter and fibrous, and the bluing cervix turns shades of gray, who will be no more than a moan, little person about whom?

Wake Up Wake Up Wake Up   Liv dreams she sits up,
rests her head against a

moan

little person

flake away desire. dissolve congested rock. underneath it is impossible not to glean. here is more than any drama can bear. spare is the room you would enter. soured are the hours you would pass. Dearest, living is beneath you. infested as it is by our nostalgic narratives of hope. here exists for itself alone. as your form passes through. stay your soul in mine. keep your room. my womb. as hermitage. these hours now are ours. but swear you will turn back.

otherwise   and deep

disappointment

Wake Up Wake Up Wake Up

she keeps waiting for this time to be

waiting for the time to be

Over breakfast Liv tells Erland she dreamed Ersatz dead, a miscarriage, and that he, Erland (Don't look at me that way), was red-faced, embarrassed about something in a goat-infested place.

Oh, yes, there was blood and breasts and moans and deep disappointment. Then, wake up, wake up,   I remember.

The HEart That She Holds

On the hemorrhaging spread on which sense rests Liv knows she strays, is straying into. There are a trillion reasons to go forward, to say "yes" and let the body lead.

Each hour that passes occludes the life within her, a fusion she feels the body needs. Is pregnancy the thing happening or the reason? When Liv says, *I am so sorry . . . I am so sorry that . . .*

she is willing herself forward into the birth she fears because she fears the regret of before, as if all loss must be repaid, as if a body spoilt will spoil itself in spite, tick tocking toward barren.

Minute to minute she is released from doubt and then certain she is misled. She avoids her thoughts, circles wide, maneuvers toward the void where what matters is what is.

7:23 am

Erland

who presumed birth, is taken to tomato red. He feels, obliquely,
his own need, as if it were greed to resent life being walked
away from. What is left to him understands little—Is their child
poor company, cadaver of a incompetent cervix, discard of a
drawn lot? Is he a burden on her uterine muscle? assuming too
huge a room? This is it: a whole possible embodied by Liv and
she now not caring, fearing, though nearing to meet it. In thought
the thought is barely tolerated, ushered out, and still

oh, Liv,

must you insist on rot in the plot to continue? Must you turn life
on its head, inverse the process, live its evil?

Liv,

must you kill life's will toward its one true recognition of joy?

Liv,

oh, Liv.

Fruitless Still Life

Ideally (so already never) what they desired, sired, is a love that
would flood everyday fears communicable: each broken step,
open depth, blackened call, searing grasp, oh ruined cell—but
it's a retarded and retarding love that frets. Though fret love will
until ill or illy suited to protect the Xed-in soul of another (as if
any other could be shielded by any him or her), it hems, it haws,
it coughs its part, it peters out, it does. Seen for itself, love must
face regret—material tent held over (though never cemented),
a wish thrown far, some ink to document the days, record a birth
outworn, and, torn to tears   other times.

3

A short narrative of hand and face entitled

Proximity of Clock to Lock

In the marriage, not able to anticipate how they would feel when baby Ersatz was born, they made decisions now about how they would make decisions then.

He was biting his cuticle.

She pulled his hand away from his face.

He was biting his cuticle.

And this seemed reasonable in the midst of insurance forms: plan A with a ninety-dollar deductible, plan B without.

He was biting his cuticle.

Because the system had a doctor inside and a doctor outside—

His tongue lifted the sliver of skin liking the feel. his tongue lifting. his teeth creating a list of tears. little rips in the claims the birth would make. errata on his hands. were they the wrong hands? botched and reddening.

He was biting his cuticle.

She pulled his hand away from his face: kept and salted terrain:
in the doldrums. characterized by calms. at a depth capable of
stasis:

He saw that where sperm dried this morning his skin looked
ashen. flaking. as if it were the dead of winter and he did not
care. as if the taste of laughter were showing itself. and he did
not care.

He was biting his cuticle.
(What?) (You know what.)

Proximity of Inner to In Her

More flesh of their flesh? What was it that they wanted?
In the days they were not careful. too much fluttering to not
respond. not reenter. not laugh and not swallow the laugh.
what was it they wanted?

He does not call out. except with his eyes.

He passes each moment and knows it is never that. never the
moment calling. it is he who calls out. awakening each moment.

Blink and the link is gone.

Blinded, she wonders away, increasingly encased by the
projected angled scar of a perhaps C-section. Surely it too will
cost: a newer fear in the cut or did she cut a fear. a thought spill.
involving the womb's pace. its face.

Then the anterior view:

She's turning back to look you in the eye. wry-neck bird, Ersatz.

A groove in her palm says a boy will be born. says they will not
be blind forever though the marriage would cry "no,"

though the marriage would cry "please,"

and always their sighs would be the sighs that mattered.

When a breath comes would they let go in relief?

This figured equation takes Liv awry down the broad hallway
(we live in each other, hold each other up like able tables). she
asks the bathroom to be her escape. below being. in the still.
moment the house chokes. in the gnashing of low. oh blue
violence of true. in tolerable decision. decide a child beneath
the eye. unborn infant in the still-illumined mind.

The moment wakened. awakening soul of. cape to warm herself.
in she steps from the swarming arms of her own insides where
a ticking sticks to the mind like a drip a room away. urethral
resistance lowers. a stream sprays the bowl.

She lets the tissue fall, wondering, Is the new always a form of a
truce? a bruising?

Proximity of Opens to Person

All morning sickness is and rushing across a bridge in
downpour . . . saturated . . . she could not reconcile . . .

it is that . . . the moment and the rock has been lifted . . . that
motion . . . a movement . . . milky gossamer worming up through

the moist . . . that semblance and emerging on the ridge . . .
conscious consciousness . . . its overproximity and tangling

being . . . though the surface is meant to be the concealer . . . its gaze
borne out of a glossiness poured in . . . pushing out away from

then the journey (step aside) does not show . . . not the journey
not the desperation . . . choke down . . . digest the adjacent

disturbance . . . preoccupied fault in the surging swell . . . it is that
needing to be subdued, subsumed, sub . . .

merge the "out." The mouth, she thought, intends to open
wide . . . paddling, paddling

to the surface under marmoreal skies . . . inarticulate before
a swallow . . . the thickening throat . . . bleached-out varicose . . .

choked back in order . . . in order that saliva . . . its silvery sick
slippery sickness slips . . . to surface up . . . dissolve ingested.

It would be blue that makes a way, she knew . . . even here . . .

if its vertical sliver took hold of "sky" and "light" . . . though
swallowed and within . . . inside the drenched

sickness . . . purling this bridge, their way across . . . and the three-
o'clock children . . . the boys . . .

a small one turning . . . to grin into the soaked ridiculous . . .
streaming is his hair plastered against . . . his wetness lit. . . .

The taste of rain, if I were thirsty, would be as faith at sunrise,
she says . . . before folding to ordinary breathing. . . .

Why? he asks. It often rains . . . now . . .

and now . . . this thickening in her throat . . . gray . . . rays arise from
the blue . . . it would be gray that calls the rain

she knew . . . even if the vertical sliver . . . blue . . . she could not hold
back . . . the color that is . . . its silvery slick . . . saliva

sickness slipped . . . surfacing up . . . It would be blue that makes
a way, she knew . . . then blurting out . . . thickly smeared. . . .

And there's no getting to, she tells him. . . .

No getting to, he repeats . . . in the falling off . . . of rain and
persons stirred to absurdity . . . his laugh in use. . . .

Don't you see, we've been made unacceptable for
entrance . . . pulled into nature . . . soaked thin within its chill,

inhabiting simply its age . . . Like a dripping leaf? he laughs. . . .
A dripping leaf, she sighs.

A dripping leaf folded to fever's will.

Proximity of Stuck to Tuck

Liv's own mother had the smell beneath her nails. It convinced her that is how she lost him. He would cover his lips with her hand: the nail seeping the scent of infant. a dry hollowing of appetite. The forgotten kiss—

resigned. dismissed. Finally and once Liv's mother asked,

Why have you let go of my hand?   Her father answered,

I was supposed to go and now I am late.

4

A short speech entitled

Proximity of Weary to Wary

As she could not applaud the mothers and fathers, their slithering climb, Liv was there ah-ah-ahing the wrinkled faces, 768,946,830,137 units of DNA, coded for survival mostly. The gallery yelled, *"Ask us how we plead."* And the official, the official said, *"Girl, let's not lose sight of why you shy from them. Let's not forget what stalls you and who, who is responsible, you in that feeling billions feel, envenomed sense of enormous, and yet, standing there, stumped, considering, though dimpled still."*

Is the approaching moment ever not demotic? Each desire, however knotty, hormonally generated. To surrender the outcome is to lose the script, to let the ridicule, ridiculous, and therefore the joy take us elsewhere. In our pregnancy, our public showing of much private resolve, every hand listening for the kick assumes bliss exists. And, in consequence, the blurring landscape is set against speed. It holds so much of our lives, in accidents, departures triumphant, arrivals. The night, the fog, a white moss of melted dew or mossy green of soaked leaves. You needn't shuffle. There needs to be seen the chance in a thing, the possible embrace, not simply the spiderweb lace (ugh) lining the ouch. Be bop, Ersatz, when we approach

be not distracted by grinding back molars, milky shakes drawn up in a straw, there reside butterflies off kilter in all. It is clear, no tingle without intention survives. We mean to be good.

Eight Sketches

After Lily Briscoe's Purple Triangle

in hope that the mother and child in hope that the mother and
child in hope that the mother and child in hope that the mother
and child in hope that the mother and child in hope that the
mother and child in hope that the mother and child in hope that
the mother and child in hope that the mother and child in hope
that the mother and child in hope that the mother and child in
hope that the mother and child in hope that the mother and
child are meant to be
      an exertion into
      need relating to

  transparent to

                    released to being
         without surfeit: nothing, no moment in exceed

(to land as inception, beginning now, despite the smoldering
other surfacing up to smother, to begin again, newly to be, and
in being, belong

But

it was that
that that she feared:

a mother in fear

wadded together:
simultaneously unable to hold off while holding

(to separate from the surface, to throw oneself into relief but not
to land as shadow, not to emerge subject to intersection, subject
to collision

```
                                              shadow
                                              ed




er      y       ly      ing     iness
```

(the damaged image absorbed to appear, the exemplar seen
and felt as one, having grown thick in the interior, opens on
to surface and is the surface reflecting its source

a portrait

bruised

triangular pelvic-shaped   a purple
darkening so much

                    too much

                                shadow

(triangulated so that the obstruction holding shadow is the self
obtruded, reflecting its surface, surfacing up its source, true

A face   silenced by its own resignation to its roots.

A face as mother, a shadowing other, an unyielding
surface in waste and worse—purple

from the purpling bruise in falter, unsteadily altering.

(in perpetual addition, nearing loss, the absorption blocking the
greater prominence, itself blocking itself

awakening

nausea—

a sea she bares in herself for herself because it takes all
to silence

the other becoming the silent call

(until the thawing, impregnated, erupts the surface, its call
dissolving to reflect the ruptured surface reflected

the conceived "we" a bruised purple surface
erupting into

hush she hush she

hush

shush   rushed within

        to shatter the surface that is the self

(a surface, within itself triangulated, blocking the self until
pulled back tautly, until bits of hue and cry thrust

shush

                                    owning its own pulsing

                                    yielding

a hurt progeny to a live evil living hymn within

(the surface, as in occlusion, pooled in accordance with, given its inside meaning, lies floored within its call and is the damaged beauty of what?

. . . of what? God help us, what?)

About the pregnancy . . . should we tell the parents?
You mean before they tell us? Maybe they'll think I've had
    breast implants.
Which reminds me, will the baby be your only customer?
I always suspected you were the type to take milk out of the
    mouths of babes.
The lowliness of my tongue confesseth . . .
Jesus?
Augustine. Saint.

5

of course. of course.

Here is a log . . . a black log of soaked bark like floating fur.

"What kind of log is that?"

"No log . . . a woman."

"A woman's body? Oh, right."

This in an instant . . . less than a minute . . . and yet, now, something out there, out of sight, rapaciously frowning at life. We can't shake the natural course of things. It's our own problem—the damming in the human condition. We are, after all, well aware.

The thing in play (Act I)

A world outside this plot prevents our intermission from being
uninvolved—a present, its past in the queue outside the toilet,
in each drink dulling the room. Hence our overwhelming desire
to forgive some, forget others. Even so, we are here and, as yet,
I cannot release us to here, cannot know and still go on as if all
the world were staged. Who believes, "Not a big mess but rather
an unfortunate accident arrived us here." Our plot assumes
presence. It stays awkward, clumping in the mouth: I shall so
want. And this is necessary time. Only now do we respect
(or is it forget) the depths of our mistakes. There often rises
from the fatigue of the surface a great affection for order. Plot,
its grammar, is the linen no one disgorges into. Excuse me.
From that which is systemic we try to detach ourselves; we cling
to, cellophane ourselves into man-made regulations, so neatly
educated, so nearly laid: *He maketh me to die down.* But some
of us have drowned and coughed ourselves up. The deep
morning lifts its swollen legs high upon the stage. Some wanting
amnesia float personified abstractions. Some wash ashore, but
not into the audience, not able to look on. Help me if who you
are now helps you to know the world differently, if who you are
wants not to live life so.

Still in play (Act II)

On the street where children now reside, the speed limit is 25.
Green owns the season and will be God. A rain, that was, put
a chill in every leaf, every blade of grass. The red brick, the
asphalt, cold, cold. The front step, the doorknob, the banister,
the knife, the fork. A faucet opens and the woman, Liv, arrives
as debris formed in the sea's intestine, floating in to be washed
ashore and perfumed. In time she opens her mouth and out
rushes, "Why is the feeling this? Am I offal? Has an unfortunate
accident arrived me here? Does anyone whisper *Stay awhile*, or
the blasphemous *Resemble me, resemble me?*" Those watching
say with their silence, That is Liv, she has styes on her eyes,
or she needs to forget the why of some moment. She doesn't
look right. She is pulling the red plastic handle toward her,
checking around her. She's washing, then watching hands, feet
and shouting *Assemble me. Assemble me*. She is wearing shoes
and avoiding electrical wires, others, steep drops, forgotten
luggage. Those are her dangers. She cannot regret. A hook out of
its eye, she's the underside of a turtle shell. Riveted, and riven,
the others stare, contemplating the proximity of prison to person
before realizing the quickest route *away from* is to wave her on.
They are waving her on. Liv is waved on. Everything remains
but the shouting. A cake is cooling on a rack. Someone is
squeezing out excess water. Another is seasoning with salt. The
blacker cat is in heat. A man sucks the mint in his mouth. The
minutes are letting go. A hose is invisible on the darkened lawn.

Musical interlude (Act III)

A certain type of life is plot-driven. A certain slant in life. A man sucking his mint lozenge. He is waiting for the other foot to drop: his own, mind you. In a wide second he will be center stage.

His song will be the congregation of hope. He will drain his voice to let Liv know she cannot move toward birth without trespassing on here: To succumb to life is to be gummed to the reverberating scum seemingly arrested.

Erland knows Liv is as if in a sling, broken in the disappeared essence, the spirit perhaps: catfoot in a moist soil, at the lowest altitude or simply streamside, though seeming fine.

He knows he too, sometimes, is as if below, pained, non-circulatory, in an interval, the spirit perhaps in an interval. But then frictionized, rubbed hard—

sweet-life-everlasting, he is singing softly beneath his meaning in the sediment of connotation where everyone's nervously missing, so missed. His melody is vertical, surrendering suddenly to outcome, affording a heart,

recalling, after all, another sort of knowing because some remainder, some ladder leftover, is biddy-bop, biddy-bop, and again. His voice catches. It feels like tenderness beckoning and it is into her voice, rejoicing.

In mortal theater (Act IV)

blessedly the absolute miscarries

and in its release this birth pulls me toward that which is without
comparison. in the still water. of green pasture. Lord and Lamb
and Shepherd in all circumstances. daylight in increase. always
the floating clouds. ceaseless the bustling leaves. we exist as if
conceived by our whole lives—the upsurge. its insides. in all
our yesterdays. moreover

asking and borne into residence. the life that fills fills in a world
without synonym. I labor. this is the applause. This—mercy
grown within complexity. and in truth these lies cannot be
separated out: I see as deep as the deep flows. I am as willing
as is recognized.

I am.

am almost to be touching

6

Painting after the death of Virgina Woolf entitled Beached Debris

Beached debris I

The painting, Liv knows, has to be truer than its reflection.
The subject must be erased though the painting is saturated
by what was felt, what was seen by the erased face. Liv's
eyes have looked so hard the painting turns to acknowledge
the space surviving Woolf's departed face. In the landscape
Woolf's body grows silence as Liv approaches the
recognition beckoning her. Then Liv is and inside Woolf's
nature; her experience is the death, which is the debris.

She experiences and is herself as beached debris. of course.
of course.

You, she says to the quiet reflecting Woolf's absorbed face,
you are a log . . . a black log of soaked bark like floating fur.
And though Liv approaches willingly the gaping enigma
smoke-shading the muddy bank, its eroding shoreline, her
darkened heel, penciled in, relinquishes movement.

indrawn mound   within surrender   mounts
    its own shadow   dull hush (squatter within)
           the tide not wanting her

neither in heaviness   nor solace   though wind
              slopes   her surface
           bandaged bone shut in
to equivocate   to abandon
       forced conclusion flensed by nature

           in quenched light a lulled while
              covering to gray the flesh
                   of tumulus

and still the irreducible already truth

       quietly stains each lithic band
until all was the same made the same soul

Beached debris I

Beached debris II

Or is the self (she paints) insulated from itself because it has been handheld, occupied by everyone?

"What kind of log is that?"
"No log . . . a woman."
"A woman's body? Oh, right."

She paints the River Ouse darker than its flow, its cloud-lined exterior housing all that has rested in Woolf's erased face.

She paints lightest the wind she breathes into. Beyond the self, the land swells into an existence that is its own battle.

Its largest stone—for her pocket—ensuring a river can slip beyond her breath, out of her mouth

beneath her reach. beneath her heels, this drowning, her own debris.

: still activity a foot and three steps from where lowered
lids close contemplating what was ever seen so ever
inclusive though spoken of: still activity solidly spilling
that which is ever a spill and a nearer fear freestanding:
its direction somatic or inert now years and too much
in each eye shuddering sky: each shudder and the I as a
strayed to ashen link losing to the calm oneiric: and still to
scratch the saturated: to touch to retouch and surface: a face
effaced riverine: embanked and soaked through: streamed
surface. its surface through. as if a next were beginning:

Beached debris II

Beached debris III

I think I am open to experiencing all drowning but I remain
suspicious of landscape that is a mental rehearsal set down to
wash recognition out of mind. I see there is meant to be plot,
a burial, but the beginning of reflection should have fewer
maybes and tension should exist between the bank (our solidity)
and the river (our dissolution). Then one could move on as her
erased face has moved on. As it is, the view here is stifling.
Wherever I look, because a body is its loss all over, I begin to
feel the same loneliness lurks, the same flooding always in need
of release. You ask, *Should one allow the drowning?* Art
persists where emotion should stall—in an overwhelming,
certain end. Her landscape, in waves, held me strangely from
inception: *"Now far off down the river I hear the chorus. . . ."*
There, each step into silt is a complicated retention performed
by one woman's body in action with its reflection. Stunned into
proximity, wet and weighted down to "we," loss in aggregation,
slow-moving, heavy. What difference? And yet, natural should
be all spaces I am pulled into—spaces to exist in. I don't want
always to be thinking, Where does this flooding come from?

To be within the encounter, at the mercy of

Where only the injurious is echoed

A moment in difference between sunlight and shadow

And what indifference would make if it worried

Sink of surface sinking the surface spewing

What difference when above bits are thrown out of a star

And yet, that other neutral stabbing, dioxin-damaged

Where by-products inhabit but can't be handled, handheld

What difference to the outcome

Rose blackening earth in varying transparency

Until a surface of chlorine ashes retarding the slough

Until the surface, defoliating, embraces its shadow

Dense indifference within traced trees

Bleached shrubbery: effaced no longer and still

Loss in aggregation, slow-moving, heavy, grave matter

Being subsumed subsequent to green, salt

Beached debris III

Beached debris IV

A reflection unclotted (she decides) is a low-zipped hue, a bare midriff against the newly dug slow surge. From her hand, rifling through, then whirring back, comes an old "I"

in its downstream portrait. On her canvas, prone, fur-drenched so diverted from eruption, is a woman's body holding uncalmly steady.

One and a half centimeters in diameter is her breath. Liv sculpts it, scrapes at its coagulated surface. She is paralyzed in herself, and several inches deep into before the image is swiped by a missed stroke. The brush too heavy suddenly, or slipping her left foot in and out of its sandal, she sees herself, recalls a self extinguished of person, in excess. *Lost in darkness and distance*, she quotes, *though neither adamic nor* . . . And yet, still hideous is this soul splitting its dermis, a bloated sac pressurized into moments of debris, though clouded over, sprayed by the violence of its stream, its unmeshed chilliness.

Mechanically, Liv applies a cold cloth to clot Woolf's drips, considers the pale browns bleeding at their seams as a saucy spurring on of such unslakable resemblance.

Affixed extension of loss in thought whispering,

crouch here o damaged tender, cycle . . . cycle through
until the self sets, and is bound to a regular contract
with eroding environs yielding . . .

and still dimming, easily as any sunlit pattern, with this
difference: the low ceiling compresses, harbors bands and
sheets, plates of bone: gasps, occupy, occupy the hurt
articulation cross-hatched into this shallow space: murmuring
face, facing:a banked stamina called: I, I, I

undiminished, and the beached floral, and the ochre——

Beached debris IV

Beached debris V

Then, more reasonably, Liv wonders, Is failure the feeling
drowned though all is still surfacing where flesh meets air?
Is the body in landscape mirroring itself?
Does the outside own more than its atmosphere?
Or is the portrait reflecting her insides on the surface?
Is sky, and sky in water, naturally imbrued if reflecting in her?
How to separate an interior out?
How to keep from polluting one in the other?
How to stay in and out of it?

"What would the world be without 'I' in it?" (Virginia Woolf)

within, running down, charcoal-laden
weight as dusk in density
physically roaring because extended
all over: left to knots of hue: tarred light: unheard and
inquiring into: obliteration in the anonymity of wind in
wind

storm: only and
within: never: not now: newly

ever:

oh, to be sole.

Beached debris V

Beached debris VI

Suddenly she would have all reflections living; each brushstroke
staying unprotected, occurring . . .

her bone-bare flesh, in roused solemnity, absorbs all drainage
nature creates for balled is the exposed soul supplementing her
fleshing out into the tight broken plot she bears. Only her
boundaries are rufescent. Their softest illumination splitting to
form a calm absolute. Here is landscape promising a voice
without moisture, hard scab of powdered breadth, riddling days
with residue. And, even closer, filed down by loosening strokes,
merging into atmosphere determined by bandagelike gestures,
is the I's muscular floor below this bank's undescended pools.

what ground was   settled long ago   a vanishing link &
gillery where surface plummeted   *there, there*

in the troubled gaze raining gutted streams a widening
self evolves having gulped until the brown of ground is
the blood of face   *where in the sweet morning*

can the self arise   *and time   its complexity*
                                 while waking   throughout

be made to bend to a quiet?

Beached debris VI

But then the brush that seams her hand—its nylon hair pressed horizontally to mirror the ready frailty attaching to the glimpsed ersatz soul realized—is put down.

(Entrance into the furrowed brow,

carbonated mineral slipped in,   astir, fizzy, pop, and still

the tummy is shatterproof, like the isolating quiet that sends her
heartbeat through her hands to the migrained eye in glare. What

she calls "inevitable" the painting names depression's long

stare, its lowering ceiling, the body's rangy strokes, coalescing
with such longing. She says that which she doesn't mean
because how can she say "I am afraid of myself" to all that is

a part of the self? If the world hurls, how to insist, I am not as

the drowned, a mouth phlegm-filled, a swollen belly filling with
earth's fuel, when the drawn feeling, a dark stain positioning,

is that? The interest is not with the dissolved, and yet dissolution
surrounds, is a feeling in its duration. It observes its own density
and is the constituted dissolved toward solidity. To this refuse,

casting its shadow from flesh to canvas, she says, no. But see,
the debris is the self within the trace, then the tide is the general
condition implicated. She is afraid of herself.

Always the unborn answers,

This bank is armored, unbroken without exception, in its delicacy it acts as distraction to the flood that is joy in its earliest hints. After birth, I will perpetually stir. We will swirl together in this. Still, I know it is not pleasing, never pleasing to see our protection trembling.

7

Liv's View of Landscape 1

By landscape we also mean memory—the swept under.
covered over. skin of history. surfacing blue violence of
true. echoing from there. to here.

the depths absorbed to surface. barring the busyness of
flow. urging us toward our cravings. our mouthfuls
crashing over lips.

as our pulled-down soul glances itself as not solved
for. though brimming to fill the gaps fetching forward.

I am all of me feeling I am in constant paraphrase.
loosely. without the fence of time. in time losing to form
absorbed. swiftly caught

by my own resistance to the completed sacrifice to
the long line arriving me. bringing everything I mean.
unmistakably personal. to this same feeling of loss. lost

far from here though I am here aiming. though every
plot has prodded. each driven drama digested by this

world. a dawning giving back so much to the self. in
reflection darkening so much. the day might call it night.

In Play

I am beginning to lose myself, Liv persists.

Fix your face, a tree suggests.

The lines on my face are of the waves originally,
Liv explains.

I see you no matter who, says a cloud.

Still to speak of loss is like dusting a thought much
farther away . . . farther than the moment the atmosphere
cries, I am lost though I am here.

Liv's View of Landscape II

By landscape we mean also failure to resolve a life
sliced horizontally between living and diving.

The breath surrendering the cold in its mouth. I call to
you who. I call to you

like ice in rain to arrive beyond knowing. to have
explained. and still to find the art mist-filled.

in chill lining solitude. giving expression to the lost in
the self lost to the self of another claim.

How is the rain not I?
How is her river not I?
Am I only as . . .

. . . the surface seems.

Time We Know Is Fluid but in All Ways We Are Drawn into a Feeling of Solidity

All that I feel, says the ice,
seems all that I will ever be.

The sun waits, sighs the rain. *You can't stay.*

Of course, says the ice.

Each time, thinks the ice.

Each time and all of us so loosely based.

The Room Is a Fountain in Experience

Though a previousness, cushioned by dark, aggregates the room
(for there is no disparity),

a room is brought into existence, the activity of—

Here Liv is letting herself feel as she feels, her will yielding to
streams, the lyric field of her everyday depths.

Her presence is. It's come along, is lost, is loss, is wallside
reconciling: can I love now please?

Or in inclusion she bursts into a hood of tenderness: the body's
anguish and flesh and all reflected in the absorbed atmosphere
soaking her being,

then the self feels deeper the depicted insistence engaged, its
essential nest, its scape—

And always and each contiguous thought, approaching the
distance, augments. Viewed against, the mind reshapes and here
is refuge without its tent.

All that's resolved plots against her dividing self, binding her as
if any intervening space is recess for

her grave, an equivalence overlaying presence. Can I love now
please?

Interpretive Commentary

I see you no matter who, says the cloud.

And Liv, still pregnant, having inherited enjambic surprise while knowing what hangs on is never enough, need not be mediated though the struggle in plot against plot lands unsteadily with everything and more is needed. The shape she takes embraces her steadiness thereof, and yet, and frail? and less?

The doggy shouts,

What counts? I see what matters, matters of . . . yes, matters me.

Shellfish. No . . . approach it. Selfish. Oui.

Knock. Knock.
Who's there?
Who cannot be.
Who cannot be who?
Who cannot be known beforehand, fool.

Or Passing the Time with Some Rhyme

Too much within—close the garage, reset
the alarm, let the eye in the world coo.
The River Ouse flows on no matter what
or who gets caught as its debris. She sits
in Le Café for once not distracted
by boo, its bark. She sits rudely sunglassed,
blue silk cascading off her tumultuous
tummy. Honey, are you happy? You there,
indiscriminate, in your loosened dress
skirting sidewalks. You there, flirting across
each shop window though a pastel broach moos
powdered jade, asking, Are you happily—
oh bovine, oh babe—are you happily
charmed? For this world, oh this whorl is a woo.

Interlude

Just then the woman at the next table said her pregnancy made her feel less lonely and Liv sat up, leaned forward. She removed her sunglasses. The two in conversation looked over and the taller one shifted unconsciously away from Liv's direction. But already Liv was forgotten. The shorter, pregnant woman said again how her pregnancy was a way to put the self she did not like behind her. *Everyone loves me now,* she whispered, and grinned. She lived for this new self the world loved. Expectant, sacred, she felt special. People smiled at her all the time all times of the day. The pregnancy was like an enormous campaign, "Hello, World!" She liked the world better now that the world loved her. The pregnant woman and her many words expressed this thing. Liv leaned back in her chair. Their conversation had taken a disappointing curve. Not concerned with how much the world loved. Not concerned. The world did not love. Or the world is love. Either way, and yet . . . there had been a beginning. . . . *The pregnancy has made me feel less lonely.* The start had startled her. She held her found thought like a photograph before her. A beautiful photograph? A true photograph? Real? Was it a real photograph? The "true real." She recalled the phrase from college, the phrase but not its meaning. And wanting a soft sweet, wild strawberries perhaps, Liv left a twenty-dollar bill on the table and walked by the other pregnant woman and her friend out onto the sunlit. She caught her reflection in a shop window—a pregnant woman approaching. *Less lonely?* She considered. Erland, she said aloud, we will be three in a sea of billions. *Less lonely.* First Liv. Then, sometimes, wife. Sometimes mother. Sometimes wife and mother. And still Liv. Liv in guilt. Liv in feeling. Liv creating herself. Liv alone.

Are you awake?

I could be.

I was thinking . . .

Yes?

I was thinking about something I saw today.

Do I have to guess?

A pregnant woman.

You are the pregnant woman.

Umm . . . but I saw another. I saw her from the side, in profile. Her
stomach really seemed other . . . not essentially her at all . . . not
something eventually able to substitute for anything, just
someone else approaching.

And this was a liberating moment?

In that heimlich way that allows the step out of this self into
myself. Does that make sense?

You mean you saw the child for the first time as other than
yourself and knew the feeling as true?

Exactly . . . not as a corruptible extension but as that person
over there. *Apart from* though *a part of.*

Congratulations.

You're sweet.

That same night Erland pressed his ear to Liv's belly.

What do you hear? Liv asked.

Not you, Erland answered. Not you.

8

A few minutes entitled

In Thought Rather Than Conversation

Liv, herself alerted by the minutes accumulating, was watching
Erland sidetracking his morning   by
examining
Johnson & Johnson baby oil, castile soap, safety pins, Vaseline,
pacifier, talcum powder, quilt, this and this other thing within
his paralyzed sense of domesticity.

He was feeling fettered by their inlaid grooves . . . "afterward,"

its freewheeling presence,   molecularly structured,
dimensions variable (for as yet unknown).

Once his present geographically shoved up against consequence
—as in a simple minute created a tacit connection between
"held" (the moment happened or was happening) and "hold" (a
new present condition, an intimacy that smudges splitting up the
seconds molecularly)—like a single eye he was taking a tunneled
look.

And uncertain, unable to hush that feeling he wants instead to
dispossess, to stop from leaking, he'd say he wishes to engineer
"it" differently because he is certain the days in fear, the days
Liv is unable to prove she is alive, will arrive. Then,

even then, with the child in his arms the storm will be an
immunity disrupting, an octopus drizzle.

All this and all the while Erland is unaware Liv is here.
I am here. I am here.   What she sees makes her look

younger.

What are you thinking?

He winks and she catches that glint as a glimpse of a cool day.

Proximity of Accrue to Rue

The day started with Erland grumpy, Liv struggling to shrug. His surface was numb without. It put itself entirely within itself and now could not look on from the distance.

This is for you.
I don't want it.
It's for you . . . take it.

His left hand gripping the car wheel, Erland watched his wedding band, its light play. For him distance was a missing surplus, an obscure longing though it is there in the way of. For him distance was the obstruction: defined, shaped, already posited within.

You know . . . about the baby . . . Is this about your baby?
Our baby.
What we wanted . . .
What did I say?

Liv sat beside Erland gathering Ersatz's heartbeat in the palms of her hands. She thought Erland felt continuity was determined in thought, not through experience. And could she blame him? she who still thought, feeling the blister at the join of her thighs, that the breaking, its sudden rinse, would blunt though she was happily inclined, upstretched, persuading the sunlit backdrop.

Do you think when E is born we will be overcome by fear?
Fear of what?
Endings, dying.
You mean a fear of death . . . our child dying, being hit by a car or
     something. . . .
Umm.
I don't know. Just now I was thinking of us being caught in our
     marriage, in our house, on our street for the rest of our lives.
Till death do.
I'm serious . . . our future seems slowed down . . . in a daze because
     of the baby.
Umm . . . loco-motion.
No . . . listen . . . the baby. We'll be up nights unable to work. E will
     be crying. And you . . .

Then the facing distance is the destruction, its construct an
obstruction: defined, shaped, already posited within. The surface
already that that is missing, a loss though it is there in the way
of.

I read this interview where the video artist Bill Viola said that
     when his baby was born, at the actual birth, he understood
     humility for the first time.
Fragility . . . he said fragility and death. . . .
Maybe you are feeling it already . . . how fragile everything
     is . . . our identities, time, our marriage.
You really must be less cheerful.
No . . . I don't mean our marriage exactly, but change.
And what if the change is bad?
We make it better.
I see . . . it's that simple. . . . "A headache could happen to anyone."
Clinton?
Hejinian. Lyn.
Umm . . . the midwife's door is over there. Number 45.

On this day the land slides, bosoms out, soaked through by the impregnated. Absorption swells to brimming but this is not that—not brine crumbling a bloated shoreline.

Proximity of Posed to Exposed

Brush handle between her teeth, she stretches. And then, the jolt—a kick? a swing? she couldn't know. Stepping back, she re-encounters the painted moment, the part that is still wet, below his right eye, the entire cheek area, chin and shoulder. She is painting his unknown parts still in outline though grown to encompass the matter of a small boy, his boy on his shoulders; their marriage swelling into the torso of son, a smaller frame, its surprising weight, difficult of course, a chance of course.

Where the paint darkens lives the year his voice broke into being a thing having lost its step, stumbling wildly, trying to catch itself, never falling, ever fallen, and never settled, yet deepened. He was a man, a man to be a father. That close to his face, and out of sense, throughout his boyish thoughts were spoken by the man's voice coming from his lips, that voice, sure, yet tentative—at every turn a subtler tone floating before him, running through, a river running through. He found himself coughing before he spoke as if to bridge the break before— *Hello.*

Liv, stepping closer, paints into the space between his lips.

Watching her, Erland, feeling at a certain disadvantage, asks
from across the room, *What have you painted? Is he a piece, as in a
segment, slice; or at peace, as in tranquillity of mind? Piece or peace of mine?*

The hidden solid in the shift of our experience is a child.

This Erland tells to the portrait that is himself.

Additionally the self reflected feels himself in gradual loss.

His mind in pieces. The time soft, in despair until the colors
before him surface up from within, flood through.

He reaches through the tears rushing, blushing his cheeks.

He reaches through and in his fading becomes coated in
a moist layer of peace touching together other emotions,
a moor of feelings.

9

One Late Afternoon

yellow rind lights the lip of her glass lit by yellow rind

(Tuesday)   her voice suspends the day in itself
All day   Erland would say if he were here
(All day)   Liv says in his place

a narrow tower of sparkling liquid

Ersatz—though pressing a wound to her back—is
without the tiniest movement

enormous stillness hum of the hot-water heater   trace of a siren

Liv waits to feel a muffled swing a hand a foot pushed what was
it that she wanted whether her eyes are open or closed

the glass she holds sweats droplets slide to the tile puddle

daylight is better than nighttime dreaming a river floating
out flooding her lungs deeply in the wrestle and toss always she

wakes being pulled up sharply fighting for breath waiting to
feel a muffled swing a hand a foot pushed what was it that she

wanted whether her eyes are open or closed she waits

a lemon slice floats a lid

without within in memory the answer is a secret between life
and yet . . .

amounting to this:

Once upon a time a body ascended through aporia, doubt's doubt. Its deception is the weight of itself, is the burden of a body, is the loss in existence. Where had the self fled? To sit is never again To stand is never again To sleep is never again To breathe is never again To say is the furnace of selfish. What would the world be? Or to wish is always To want is always To breathe is always To wonder without, to brood inside a world given within, without "I" in it. But then the must, the must attempt to fill at least in part, for there is, after all, a whole other existing within, struggling to surface for milk and years in innocence, an embankment of life before trust, a faith in land scaped. And there the seeing was done, she knew she loves enough to love, to call forward the infinite in the self to love all that survives and is her, is here, all that is existence persisting in the quagmire giving way beneath surface alliances, in the soft earth, its fluid steadiness sending forth bandaged birch, relaxed floral, silvery-gray greens, a groundwork through which she speeds the path toward continuance. For she loves below the full sun the sustained sequence, the interlocking earth, an ocean of hardened water dazzling its fixed terrain of love arriving before existence in the exploited blur of her cratered understanding of our soul's intimacy within the opportunity that is life.

still the body. in its horror of explosion. stretched to house what
is not her. waiting to feel a muffled swing. a hand. a foot pushed.
what is it that she wants whether her eyes are open or closed. she
waits—
2
4
6
8

Erland took the stairs two at a time. Liv listened, contemplating the climb.

Tired?
Two tired.
What have you been up to?
I've just been sitting here thinking about Virginia Woolf.
Woolf? Really? Did she have any children?
None.
You sure?
Sure I'm sure. She didn't have any children because she was
      afraid of herself . . . of her madness.
She actually thought her depression contaminated her?
Do you, my love, think love conquers all?
Ever and never.
Then . . . "You could do so much for me if you just would."
Ahhh. . . . *As I Lay Dying*.

The Ouch in Touch

(curved to the C of fetal. positioned for warmth. her left breast in
his right hand. his elbow a shield before her belly. his breath the
heat of her shoulder. a still moistness between her legs. love of
the previous lovemaking awakened by their slightest shift

and still her belly. their child always there. a tenderness in the
way of tenderness. turning her tense.

In order to meet him. to be within and not simply that which he
enters. she imagines herself as before. a surface of want entering
its reflection.

the reflected emotion surmounting the real. surviving it.

In the Present Perfect

As a glazey substance discharges from its passage of remorse,
the soft bones of the head flex into position, all immunities
gained. Is this now the beginning of hope, now all desire
rupturing behind the milk teeth buds, within each rudimentary
breath, the extremes sensible to pain soon to cry from hunger,
from cold, a mouth soon to call out to her to call out to him?

E's heavy head moves downward, engaged, and unstopped is
the access facing into the storm maneuvered of course
to break.

And she of vascular spiders and swollen ankles and more and
more pee knows, though his balance is thin, transparent still,
his eyes will open

in the crank, in the cramp, in the crash upthrusting.

Shit.
What? What is it? Is this it?
No . . . I mean yes, but still early.
Contractions?
Contractions.
Do you feel like walking?

Proximity

Though it is false, their slow idle,
the two move below a white sky. as if dozing. dwelling in
unexpressed rain. without memory their pace slows. they ebb
and flow into emergence. finding themselves present only. a
pulsing organ of increase. no thought ahead. trusting in every
ninth minute. centimeters counting up. forcing a way through
twisting corkscrews uncoiling gain. such pain. stark revolving
echoes. stirrings within. what. what. what was it about this cold.
the still? content. called to watch. to wait. willing silence in.
inside a light too low now to take for granted. too soon wickedly
brilliant. boldly bloodied orange. nearly extinguished to dusk.
winter bare. bosky. stripped trees at bone. and here. there. frail
extensions of last spring's new branches.

(Their aim, as they stroll in places still grass-green and then
burlap brown alongside a graying, grayer river, is to walk into
each contraction, to move time through her body, its unfolding,
making its way by marking, beneath the white and soaplike
crust of epidemic scales. globules of oil. mucus shale.

the opening beyond which will be his first horizon.

. . . how many days can we hush up, how many hours? To know
ugliness and yet the beauty we are is the battlefield we live
is the body to use in favor—

The head, its face, its forgotten, finally forgotten surface, bent back,

push

the breath now in no return the breath now the breath without residence in service only now the breath now the breath bearing down,

push

the will scrambling beyond desperate, beyond tired, tiredness a will in itself craving finish, the finish of confinement,

push

as the third layer of rumpled tissue parts, in the smallest tear see the black blood of arrival. the head through. swept clear. through the inlet. cervix to exterior. crowned. demanding to be believed. received.

Here. I am here. I am here.

Erland,

Liv,

within the second all desire remains to increase such softness that emerges, to push flesh translucent until the dawn blurs the blue-edged day transporting its newer thrill. His lips are oval-shaped to receive the premier light approaching. These are bright moments, they pass through. For it is he who yawns the body distended, he who turns toward. Light of each burning bulb absorbed bejewels these corpuscles. clusters of capillaries. drizzling gems. along Liv's veined highway.

How will he feel to the touch?

With him resides the best truth in the flesh.

All hands are drawn to—

Afterword

Here.   a landscape lies somewhat loosely in her socket

scarcely exaggerated: a Mom. a Dad.
the child I am. structured the plot they lost time to

in time the knitted cap covered my eyes. or chance is fertilized
in time

then darkness is the shifting reds and yellows of daylight
(then memory is sold to decay a rot given way to demolished
though residual might in time color the day a matte orange,
the light not living then . . .)

How much heart must I swell toward you? How count desire?

All ten fingers, unclothed, were proximity. D. kissed them. M.
caught them, five at a time, between her lips.

The hard question then is answered by them a nail at a time.

What is the world without I in it? I who am nothing without plots
propping me up—

Oh, action of narrative Oh secret plan To chart To chart A small
piece of land

Innocence in no sense, anon, aground. A soul knows. Death is
not the title of its project. Tell M. so though

It's not really about__

Or surprise comes in
from the girdled shape of the third stomach, past the black wiry
to maintain a watery horizon of bubbling spit. (This explained by
the suited dudes as if M.'s depths couldn't communicate . . .

her Model having given up: her river carrying her over . . .

She was trying to come up with something: Ouse to Other)

However . . . for all the Years lived attrition is still all, all needed
though that other gave up on the bright answer and passed so
quickly beyond the umbilical, the walling flesh

M. needing Woolf for a model was stopped dead in madder hue
of the untouched look. To live her was to coop anatomy

until D. considered M. with the stars, so other

O father O mother this soul my own

Bearden, Romare (collagist, of course), said, *They're all kinds of
people and they will help you if you let them.*

Or some such. . . .

I'd never refuse. The full thickness of my tongue forces itself to
part, to call

I segue under
the rouged opening of the boneless jaw
because green clings to the leaves,
because the idea remains
fresh

All day I will record
And never convince
With such luck we

And I am
because "here" exists. I am beyond what was. In M.'s play group
somebody's mom says, *God forgive us.*

Then she says, *The one that wasn't born, the stillborn one, was
saved.* One has to be born, I say.

One has to be born and therefore, the cry I am about to emit is
hunger only, no memory in it——crowded as it is (or is it shored
simply) by heed me. feed me. raise me up.

"Honey"——her voice of iron and glass scarved, the breast a boast
requiring an image: its brown flesh, its darker nipple, hue of
hill, of path, of downward slope; a soil bouquet where earth
meets sea . . .

unfortunate that——that hurt always sounding

sucking in——
its sound a shroud in the pull of space, a distance closing, she to
me having the eye in it (D. rubs a foot meanwhile, not mine,
hers).

D.'s hand, a tap on my back, a sometimes flick of gratitude.
Answered by unswallowed drool (warmth still in it)

"sweetness"
subsiding the ear (not rhyming this time with yesteryear's fear,
torn out)

now just now nearly a breath soaring in

now out now slower slept I

in time to time

borne to a billion chances—